LA CÔTE D'AZUR

Text, photographs, lay-out and reproduction, entirely designed and created by the technical deparment of EDITORIAL ESCUDO DE ORO, S.A.

11th Edition

I.S.B.N. 84-378-1060-4

Dep. Legal B. 24885-1997

GENERAL DISTRIBUTOR FOR THE CÔTE D'AZUR: MOLIPOR
Telephone 50 72 37 (Monaco)

Part of Menton.

MENTON

Menton is a border city situated on the most easterly point of the *Département* of the Alpes Maritimes. Well sheltered against the northern winds, this city is regarded as being the warmest resort on the Côte d'Azur, and attracts a great many retired people because of the mildness of its climate. There is a substantial amount of growing of oranges, lemons, and mandarins in the privileged situation of the hinterland of Menton.

The city first came onto the historical scene half-way through the 13th century, when Charles d'Anjou passed through Menton. In the year 1456 Lambert Grimaldi, lord of Menton, was named as successor to the prince of Monaco, and he was forced to put down an uprising of his own subjects with the help of the Duke of Milan. Menton remained united to Monaco until 1848, and in 1860 it opted for incorporation into France.

The most important monument in Menton is the church of St. Michel, which was begun in the 17th century. In the chancel of the church is conserved a valuable retable by André Manchello (16th century) and numerous objects of art of which the most outstanding is an 18th-century wooden carving of St. Michael.

Other important monuments in the city are the Chapelle des Pénitents Blancs and the Town Hall building. The wedding room of the latter was decorated by the famous painter, poet and playwright Jean Cocteau. Also of interest is the Municipal Museum, whose ground floor is given over to the archaeological collections (amongst the pieces on

Detail of Menton.

display is the skull of a Cro-Magnon man) and whose first floor houses important collections of paintings. Located in the 16th-century bastion, the Musée Jean Cocteau has an interesting collection of paintings, tapestries and drawings of incalculable value.

No less worthy of mention is the Jardin Botanique et Exotique, in which there grow numerous varieties of Mediterranean plants.

At Carnival time, Menton is transformed into a hive of activity and attracts a great many visitors, especially in the course of the celebrated Lemon Festival. In the majestic Biovès gardens there takes place a great decorative exhibition of citrus fruits.

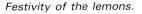

Festivity of the lemons.

Typical little streets in old Roquebrune.

*Overall view of
Roquebrune.*

Part of Cap Martin.

Overall view of Cap Martin.

MONACO

Perched atop a rock overlooking the sea, the Principality of Monaco is a first-class tourist centre, famous for its casino and the wealth which it harbours. An outstanding factor in the present popularity of Monaco has been the leadership of H.R.H. Prince Rainier and his elegant, beautiful wife H.R.H. Princess Grace, recently deceased.

It would seem that the name of Monaco derives from *Portus Monœci,* the ancient port of Hercules mentioned in several Mediterranean legends. Monaco, a haven of calm, a land soaked in sun, is an oasis of happiness. Its appearance is that of a white seabird in flight between sea and sky.

Monaco is a combination of a great city and a capital of a dream kingdom. The Principality comprises the following elements: the old city of Monaco surrounding the old château of the Grimaldi family, the port area, called La Condamine, and the the new city of Monte-Carlo, with the rock on which the Casino and various luxury hotels are placed. In the outskirts of Monaco there are preserved various relics witnessing its ancient history, as well as caves inside which the skeletons were found of the earliest inhabitants of the Mediterranean. Also preserved in the hills are the remains of the gigantic walls surrounding the ancient population centre, thus converting it into an unassailable citadel as well as a peaceful port, where, according to Virgil and Lucan "the force of Euro and Zephyr penetrate not". In 43 B.C. Julius Caesar concentrated his fleet in the port of Monaco to await the arrival of Pompey who had taken refuge in Ilyria. The German Emperor, Frederick I Barbarossa, granted to Genoa in the 12th century sovereignty over Monaco and over the whole of the Ligurian coast. It was about this time that the illustrious Ligurian family of the Grimaldis, who were Guelfs, were forced into exile when, in 1295, the Ghibellines became the wielders of power in Genoa. Francesco Grimaldi made himself master of the rock of Monaco by disguising himself as a monk so as to gain acess to the fortress. From then on the sway of the Grimaldi family over the rock increased. In 1509 Monaco came under French sovereignty, but by the treaties of Burgos and Tordesillas (1512-24), the Grimaldi family gained full autonomy for the small state, and as head of government was placed Agostino Grimaldi, bishop of Grasse, under the protection of Charles I of Spain and V of Germany, who for three days in 1529 was a guest in the château. Later, the Sovereigns of Monaco enjoyed the protection of France, but during the times of the French Revolution Prince Honorat III of Monaco was overthrown and died in exile in Paris. As a result of the Treaty of Vienna, Monaco came under the protectorate of Sardinia until 1860 when it reverted to the tutelage of France. The Principality saw a period of splendour under the guidance of

Overall view of the Principality of Monaco.

La Condamine and Monte-Carlo viewed from the rock of Monaco.

Part of the pleasure port.

Charles III Grimaldi, whose son, Albert I, consolidated relations with France. It was about that time that Monaco began to achieve fame as a tourist resort and as a cultural centre, fame which reached its peak under the present sovereign, H.R.H. Prince Rainier III.

As far as monuments are concerned, the most outstanding features of Monaco are the Grimaldi Palace, a symbol of the historical continuity of the Principality, whose rooms form an interesting museum with pictures by Giorgione, Holbein, Van Loo, Champaigne, Rigaud and other artists, Japanese furniture, valuable Venetian pieces, a fresco-painted ceiling (with a representation of "Fame with the Arms of the Grimaldi Family" in the centre), and the bed in which the Duke of York died towards the end of the 18th century. Also worthy of mention is the Napoleonic Museum where valuable archives are housed, as well as coins minted in Monaco and another collection of Napoleonic souvenirs.

The cathedral, Monaco's main architectural monu-

Monte-Carlo, the complex of the Spélugues and the Centre de Recontres Internationales (International Meeting Centre).

The façade of the Hôtel de Paris.

The great dining-room of the Hotel de Paris: the Imperial Room.

ment, rises on high ground in the city and was built between 1875 and 1884 under the supervision of the architect Lenormand. Also of interest are the Anthropological Museum, the National Museum, the Wax Museum, the Zoological Acclimatization Centre, the Oceanographical Museum, the Opera House, and the Casino at Monte-Carlo, whose years of greatest splendour began in what has come to be known as the *Belle Epoque,* and has continued to the present, offering beautiful, profusely decorated rooms, and being a magnificent example of the architectural style known as ''liberty''.

The Opera House: two views of the Sovereigns' box and the large fresco by Feyen Perrin in the background.
(S.B.M.)

*Hôtel Loews, Monte-Carlo: gambling room
(S.B.M./Loews).
Casino: the front (S.B.M.).
The Grand Prix of Monaco.*

The Cathedral.

Exterior of the Grimaldi Palace, Rainiere I, the Throne Room.

The changing of the guard at the Palace is an attractive spectacle for many people who congregate on the esplanade to get a good view of the soldiers.

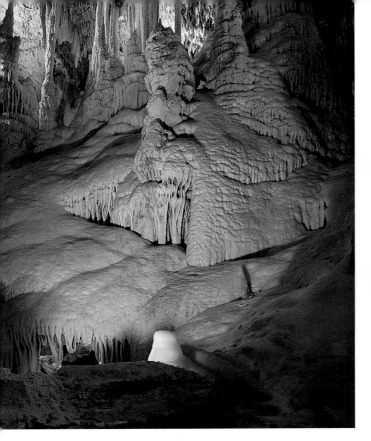

Apartments, avenues and splendid resort facilities have been built around teh beaches; a detail of Saint-Nicolas square; and a typical street of old Monaco, (p. 16).

The Exotic Garden: detail of the grottos; part of the gardens; and a view of the bay.

The Oceanographical Museum: main entrance.
Aquarium: species of marine fauna.
Exterior of the Oceanographical Museum.

Overall view of Cap d'Ail.

The streets of Eze-village.

Overall view of Eze-village.

Eze.

EZE

Eze is a town whose origins are remote. Some historians link the name of Eze with that of Isis, the Egyptian goddess; others see it as deriving from the name of *Visia* or *Avisium* given by the Romans to watchposts erected on high ground. Caesar ordered the town to be fortified. It was an old farming centre placed on top of some rocks, a veritable eagle's nest overlooking the sea from a height of 427 metres. At the beginning of the 14th century it was a Guelf citadel, and its castle was destroyed in the year 1706. The steep and narrow streets of Eze give it an air of quaintness. The most important monuments here are the old castle, a former residence of the Riquier family, lords of Eze, built in the 14th century and demolished in 1706 on the orders of Louis XIV; the Chapelle des Pénitents Blancs; and the church, which conserves a magnificent blazoned baptismal font dating from the 15th century.

Equally interesting in Eze is the Jardin Exotique, which has a great variety of plants, predominantly cactuses.

By means of a picturesque path, flanked by pines and olive trees, one descends to the lower Corniche, flanking the sea.

Beaulieu-sur-Mer: two views of the Pointe des Fourmis with the "Villa Kérylos".
Saint-Jean-Cap-Ferrat: inmates of the zoo.

CAP-FERRAT

Cap-Ferrat forms a rocky peninsula, covered with pines and olive-trees, on which there stand several luxury houses and grounds, one of them once belonging to Leopold II of Belgium. Of especial interest is the small, red-coloured, Italian-style palace, built between 1909 and 1912, and which Baroness Ephrussi de Rothschild donated to the Institut de France in 1934 for the Academy of Fine Arts. In its interior are valuable collections of works of art from the 16th to the 19th centuries. Outstanding is the collection of Sèvres porcelain, the royal tapestries from La Savonnerie and the 18th-century furniture, some of which belonged to Queen Marie Antoinette. The gardens are equally of extraordinary beauty. Here on summer evenings are held the various concerts, lectures and other cultural activities. The main garden is French in style and is surrounded by other gardens all differing in style.

General view of St.-Jean-Cap-Ferrat.

Photograph HELIFLASH

A view against the light of the bay of Villefranche; Saint-Jean-Cap-Ferrat; and Paloma-Beach at Cap-Ferrat.

The bay of Villefranche, Mont Boron and Nice in the background.

VILLEFRANCHE

Villefranche is one of the most sheltered harbours on the Côte d'Azur, and stands about 6 kilometres from Nice. It is a picturesque town, with multi-coloured houses standing out against the hillside. It has attractive stepped alleys and a covered street, the Rue Obscure, which winds its way down to the sea. Of interest are the citadel and the Chapelle Saint-Pierre, decorated by Jean Cocteau.

Part of Villefranche-sur-Mer.

Photo by Ross & Associates.

The harbour and Promenade des Anglais.

Photograph HELIFLASH

NICE

Nice is the most important town on the Côte d'Azur. The human imprint on the district dates from remote times. In the Grimaldi grotto (Nice) were found objects which certify the presence of man in the Paleolithic and Neolithic ages.

When in the 14th century Avignon came to be the religious capital of the West, the whole of Provence lived through an epoch of extraordinary importance as regards literature and art: Nice became allied with the dukes of Savoy and thus took a separate historical way from that of Provence which had become

*Nice: part of the Quai des Etats-Unis and Ràuba Capéu;
an overall view; view of the Cape; and a mosaic of Greek
inspiration in the Castle.*

The port and the Promenade des Anglais.

definitively linked to France. Nonetheless Nice did on several occasions come under the sway of France. It was annexed to France in 1793 and it was from Nice that Napoleon launched his Italian campaign in 1796. It once again came into the possession of the House of Savoy from 1814 to 1860, the year in which it was reincorporated into France, this time for good. The cession was approved *en masse* by the population of Nice in a plebescite.

Since that time Nice became the true capital of the Côte d'Azur and one of the most visited cities by people coming from all over the world. The pioneers of Nice's tourism were well-to-do English people, who arrived in Nice in ever-increasing numbers already in the first half of the 19th century, taking up residence in the Faubourg Croix de Marbre.

The light and colour of the country around Nice and other famous spots along the Côte d'Azur attracted numerous artists of universal renown. Painters like Ingres, Corot, Delacroix, Soutine, Monet, Renoir, Matisse, Picasso, Dufy, Léger, Toulouse-Lautrec, Marc Chagall, Degas, Bonnard, Utrillo and several others settled either temporarily or permanently in several places along the Côte d'Azur.

Inside the Naval Museum at Nice. ▷

The Opera House: inside and the southern side.

There were also many writers who chose Nice as a place of residence, the most important being the names of Balzac, Flaubert, Maupassant, Prosper Mérimée, Alexandre Dumas, Montaigne, Baudelaire, Verlaine, Tolstoy, the Goncourt brothers, Colette, Paul Valéry, Maeterlinck, Somerset Maugham and many others. Nice has also often been the city to which great names in politics have repaired, as well as well known figures in the world of science, finance and the aristocracy the world over. Likewise Nice has seen the birth of numerous distinguished people, amongst whom the most outstanding are the painters Van Loo and Bréa, the astronomers Cassini, Maraldi and Lascaris, the historian Gioffredo, the abbot of St.-Pons, J.M. de Gubernatis (to whom the construction of the "Villa des Arènes" in Cimiez is attributed), Frère Marc of Nice (the evangelist of Peru and Mexico), the naturalists Barla and Risso and the generals Masséna, Rusca and Garibaldi.

Nice is an attractive city on many counts. From the castle, which is the highest point in Nice, situated at a height of 92 metres, there is a splendid view over the town with the following landmarks standing out: the Quai des Etats-Unis, the Promenade des Anglais and

Hôtel Negresco: the front and the Louis XIV room.

The Masséna Museum.

An Empire style bedroom.

The room dedicated to Masséna in the museum bearing
his name.

Detail of the sumptuous staircases in the Lascaris Palace.

The old apothecary's shop in the Lascaris Museum.

the old port (built in the reign of Charles Emmanuel III of Savoy). To the left there rises Mont Boron, and to the right there spreads out the Baie des Anges and the hills on which the modern city is founded. In the distance appear the Airport and Cap d'Antibes. The Castle was in succession a trenched field for its primitive inhabitants, an acropolis to the Greeks of Marseilles, a Roman fort, and the citadel of the counts of Provence and the kings of Aragon in the Middle Ages.

The old city of Nice has a charm all of its own. It spreads out at the feet of the castle, between the Paillon and the sea. There is an abundance of palaces and pink or grey buildings. Around the Town Hall the streets are straighter and more regular, whereas on the spurs of the rock on which the castle stands there huddle charming streets, narrow, tortuous and frequently extremely steep, flanked by tall houses with flower-bedecked balconies. The most picturesque streets of this area, in which there is a predominantly half-cosmopolitan half-popular atmosphere, are those named de la Boucherie, du Marché, de la Loge, des Voûtes, and the Place St.-François to the left of which stands the Town Hall building (18th century). The Cours Saleya has its own particular charm, with its Flower Market and Opera House. The street of the Préfecture links the old Nice with the new.

The most important religious building in Nice is the Basilica of Notre-Dame, in the Avenue Jean Médecin. Architecturally Gothic in plan, its façade is reminiscent of Notre-Dame in Paris.

The cathedral of St. Réparate, built in the 17th century by the Nice architect André Guibera, is situated in the old part of the city. Its double-bodied façade is Neoclassical in style. The belfry dates from the 18th century. The interior of the church has the shape of a Latin cross, with a central dome, nave and two aisles. Conserved there are the mitre of Saint Bassus and the reliquaries of Saints Bassus and Victor.

Other noteworthy churches in Nice are the Eglise de Jésus, with its Neoclassical façade and single nave,

Nice's most modern fountain at Place Masséna.

consecrated to St. James the Apostle in the first half of the 17th century; the chapel of the Annunciation, also called of St.-Giaume; and that of the Virgin of Mercy (18th century) which has fine paintings by Bistolfi on the vault.

Special mention should be made of the Russian Orthodox Cathedral, built between 1903 and 1914 after the design of the architect Preobrajensky. Its outer structure brings to mind the Moscovite church of St. Basil. It has a nave without aisles, and displays an extraordinary wealth of ikons. In the interior of the church the most remarkable features are the fresco paintings of Designori after the drawings of Pianov-

The Basilica of Our Lady. ▷

Noah and the Rainbow, *a painting from the* Biblical
Message, *by Marc Chagall.*

sky, a fine image of the Virgin Mary, a St. Michael by
the hand of Pianovsky, and image of the Holy Saviour
(a copy of an old ikon in the Moscovite church of the
Assumption), Our Lady of Kazan, a Virgin in bronze
by Vladimir and a Saint Nicholas.

There are several interesting museums in Nice. The
œuvre of Marc Chagall on show in the museum bearing his name is of great value. The building was raised
in 1972 by the architect A. Hermant. Chagall wished
to bring together his biblical paintings in a single place
when he settled in Vence in 1950. The seventeen canvases which make up the *Biblical Message* take up
two rooms. In one of the spacious rooms are on show
twelve pictures and the five canvases illustrating the
Song of Songs can be viewed in an adjoining room. A

handsome circular room intended for lectures and
concerts is decorated by three great stained glass
windows on the theme of *The Creation of the World.*
In the Musée Masséna, which is housed in one of the
palaces in the Promenade des Anglais, is conserved
an interesting collection of old paintings. One of the
rooms displays several portraits of General Masséna
as well as pictures depicting the battles in which
Nice's glorious son took part. Of undeniable interest
are the collections of pottery, old armour, jewels,
Oriental dress, various portraits of Garibaldi, a marble

*The Russian Orthodox Cathedral containing a fine
collection of icons.* ⟩

The Virgen Mary, Consoler of the Afflicted.

The Royal Gate and access to the altar.

*Interior of the
Russian Church.*

*Monastery of Cimiez,
altar of the Church,
and the façade.*

The amphitheatre at Cimiez.

bust of Masséna (by Canova) and a statue of Napoleon. The Musée Lascaris is situated in the Rue Droite and takes up a Genoa-style building which belonged to the Lascaris-Ventimiglia family and which was the seat of the *Tribunal Révolutionnaire* from 1792 to 1794. The majestic staircase is outstanding, as are the nobly proportioned rooms with their rich decorations, together with a pharmacy dating from 1738 which is found on the ground floor and which has an interesting collection of jars and pots. Another museum of great interest is dedicated to the painter Matisse, installed in a small palace in Cimiez. It was founded in 1963 and has on display various objects which belonged to the painter together with several of his paintings, amongst which the most outstanding are those entitled *Odalisque, Portrait of Laurette, Still life,* and *Reader with yellow table.*

Also of enormous interest is the Musée de Beaux Arts Jules Chéret in the Avenue des Baumettes, in which are conserved valuable paintings of the various European schools from the 17th to the 19th centuries, with works by Van Loo, Natoire, Fragonard, etc. and a wide variety of works by 19th-century French masters: Besnard, Blanche, Cabanel, Couture and Flameng amongst others. Sculptures by Carpeaux and Rodin and important collections of Impressionist painters: Monet, Sisley, Renoir, Degas, Guillaumin; by Dufy, Van Dongen and Survage. Also on show are ceramics by Picasso. Other museums deserving of mention are the Archaeological Museum (situated in

Chéret Museum: She, *by G.A. Mossa.*

the Roman City) the Museum of Prehistory and the Naval Museum. Of the greatest interest too are the Roman ruins and the Monastery of Cimiez, in whose church there are kept valuable works of art.

Places such as the Promenade des Anglais and the hanging gardens of St. John the Baptist all contribute to sketching the attractive tourist image of Nice.

Carnival time has an especial relevance and springs from a long and brilliant tradition which goes back the 13th century. The whole of Nice dresses up and brightens during the festivities of the Carnival.

Matisse Museum: a view of the inside.

Several views of the world famous Nice Carnival.

CAGNES-SUR-MER

An interesting medieval city which stands on top of a hill. Its privileged position and the great beauty of the surrounding countryside have attracted numerous famous painters. It was in Cagnes that Renoir lived out his later years, from 1907 to 1919.

In fact there are three cities rather than one: the city standing in the proximities of the beach of Cros-de-Cagnes, the modern city of Le Logis (a predominantly commercial area) and the old city which surrounds the castle of Haut-de-Cagnes, the latter being the most interesting.

The castle and an old corner of Haut-de-Cagnes.

"Les Marina" *at Villeneuve Loubet.*

Photograph HELIFLASH

◁ *The beach of Cros-de-Cagnes.*

Entrance to the Gorges du Loup; and two views of Gourdon.

The Daluis gorges, and a natural monument called the Woman's Head.

The old fountain at Saint-Paul-de-Vence.

SAINT-PAUL-DE-VENCE

This town was an ancient fortress entrusted with the mission of defending the Var border. It is set in the midst of magnificent countryside and from the top of the walls which surround Saint-Paul there are very attractive views of the country around where cypresses, vineyards, bouganvillea and mimosas abound. The splendid medieval structure of Saint-Paul is preserved in all its purity, and offers a highly attractive sight as a town. Access to the centre is afforded through the arch of a solid tower defended by a cannon. This tower was raised in the 16th century, in the reign of Francis I, with the aim of defending the town against the dukes of Savoy. Saint-Paul was a town which in the past depended directly on the king of France.

Document history of the town begins in the 10th century. Romée de Villeneuve annexed the territory of Roquefort to Saint-Paul. When in confrontation with Louis of Hungary, Queen Joan I, the daughter of Robert de Provence, king of Naples, allied herself with Pope Clement VI, ceding to him the château of Avignon. On the death of Queen Joan, Saint-Paul came under the sway of the duke of Anjou, who confirmed the privileges of the town, and to which he added the seigneurial jurisdiction over Roquefort and Tourettes. Francis I demolished the old fortifications in 1537, and built more solid ones, thus converting Saint-Paul into a fortified site.

Of all the great monumental wealth in Saint-Paul, the church is outstanding. It was built between the 12th and 13th centuries and rebuilt in the 18th century. It is Gothic in style, with later additions. In its interior there is conserved a valuable legacy of works of art, outstanding amongst which is a splendid painting of the Virgin Mary worked in silver, dating from the 13th century; a 14th-century processional cross, a Saint Catherine from the brush of Tintoretto and a reliquary of Saint Anthony, dating from the 15th century.

In the main square is a monumental fountain built in 1850. The town has a Provençal Museum and in the famous restaurant «La Colombe d'Or» there is a fine private collection of modern painting with works by Picasso, Matisse, Dufy, Derain, Utrillo, and other famous artists.

THE MAEGHT FOUNDATION

Situated in the outskirts of Saint-Paul-de-Vence on a grassy hillside, the Maeght Foundation is one of the most interesting modern art museums existing in the world today. It is housed within a construction of brick, steel and glass which was designed by the Catalan architect Josep Lluís Sert. The museum of the Maeght Foundation (which carries the name of its recently-deceased creator) was inaugurated in 1964. The visitor is greeted at the entrance by a black sculpture, the work of Calder. Inside there are valuable paintings and sculptures by famous artists, among whom the most important are Kandinsky, Braque, Marc Chagall, Miró, Matisse, Léger, Bonnard and Giacometti.

Saint-Paul-de-Vence: typical street.

Sculptures by Giacometti in the Maeght Foundation.

Biot: the arched square; and glass craftsmanship.

BIOT

Biot is a picturesque town situated atop a hill dominating the valley of the Brague. It offers to the visitor a considerable wealth of monuments. Outstanding is its square (12th century), with fine arches and beautiful fountain. Its Romanesque church is also of interest. The doorway, dating from 1506, bears the signature of Tadeus Nigerus. In its interior there are conserved fine altar-pieces and retables from the Bréa school (1500). One of them has eight panels, depicting the Virgin of the Rosary surrounded by saints. Another has four panels, the main figure being an Ecce Homo.

Biot has deposits of clay, siliceous sand and manganese, which potters of all ages have used for the manufacture of jars and various utensils. Already the Phocaeans used to export their products from the port of Antibes. The importance of Biot has grown in the past few years as a consequence of an upturn in glass craftsmanship. Various objects, such as carafes, bottles and pitchers are made by glassmakers using age-old techniques.

Of equal importance in Biot is the production of carnations and roses.

In the small town of St.-Pierre, situated some 6 kms. from Biot, is to be found the Musée Fernand Léger, named after the great French painter, friend of Picasso and Braque, who was described by the American critic Sweeney as ''the primitive of modern times''. The façade of the Museum is decorated with a vividly-coloured mosaic and in its interior there is conserved a collection of drawings, paintings, tapestries and ceramics by Léger. In these works can be seen the artist's development from 1904 throught to 1955 and his passing from Cubism to a kind of painting which is characterised by its extraordinary expressiveness.

Valbonne: parish church of Saint Blaise; rue à arcades; and rue Gambetta.

Aerial view of Antibes and the ramparts.

Photograph HELIFLASH

ANTIBES

The town of Antibes, situated opposite Nice on the other side of the Baie des Anges, was founded by the Phocaeans in the 4th century BC. Its name is, precisely, due to its situation: Antipolis or the "town opposite" in relation to Nice. From the 5th century onwards the Greeks of Massalia established a series of trading posts along the coast, dealing with the Ligurian tribes. Antibes was a sheltered little port of call, between the bays of La Salis and St-Roch, fortified by ramparts but constantly at the mercy of any Ligurian attack. Two centuries later the town became a Roman municipality with its arsenal and parade-ground; but was subsequently destroyed by barbarian invasions.

From the 14th century onwards, France's monarchs were aware of the strategical importance of Antibes, particularly when it was on the frontier between France and Savoy. Each reign brought new improvements to the town's fortifications, which were completed by Vauban; today only the Fort Carré and the ramparts giving onto the sea survive.

In 1794 Bonaparte — charged with the defence of the coastline — established his family in Antibes, but after Robespierre's fall he was imprisoned in the Fort Carré for a time.

General Championnet, who had distinguished himself in the German and Italian campaigns, died in the town in 1800. He had asked to be buried by the ramparts of the Fort Carré; a bust to his memory stands in the Cours Masséna. Maréchal Reille (1775-1860) was

Antibes: the ramparts and the Château Grimaldi, housing the Picasso Museum.

Cros-de-Cagnes: the watery world of Marineland-Antibes.

born in Antibes and won distinction in all the Napoleonic campaigns; he later rallied to the monarchist cause and was named Marshal by Louis-Philippe.

The Château Grimaldi is reached via the narrow streets of the old town; this castle was built on a terrace overlooking the sea, its structure is that of a Roman *castrum* rebuilt in the 16th century and retaining its Romanesque square tower.

The castle now houses the Picasso Museum, with an extremely valuably collection of paintings, drawings, engravings, lithographs and ceramics by the great painter. There are also interesting archaeological items and the visitor may admire four statues by Germaine Richier on the terrace facing the sea. Other important monuments include the 17th century cathedral with Romanesque apse and transept and a magnificent retable corresponding to the school of Louis Bréa, which dates from 1515. The Archaeological Museum, installed in the St-André bastion of Vauban's fortifications, has an important collections of coins and historic ceramics. The Naval and Napoleonic Museum occupies a sturdy round tower, the Batterie du Grillon, at the south-west tip of Cap d'Antibes. Behind the church and the castle, the visitor will encounter the sea-front boulevard which is none other than the 12th century rampart, carefully conserved.

The Porte Marine ("Marine Gate") stands in the area of the harbour. Nearby the visitor will see a fountain constructed by Louis XVI in honour of General

Picasso Museum (Château Grimaldi): a tapestry by Rouault; ceramics and tapestries.

The Plage *(beach)* du Coq *at Antibes, and La Garoupe chapel.*

d'Aguillon, who restored the Roman aqueducts supplying the city with water.

Contemporary Antibes is above all a leading town as regards the production of cut flowers (roses, carnations and anemones), with nearly 800 horticultural establishments whose glass-houses occupy an area of almost three million square metres. Antibes also enjoys the distinction of having been the first place in Europe to acclimatise eucalyptus.

The adaptation of the Côte d'Azur to the necessities of tourism gave rise to the creation of a highly-reputed port for pleasure craft and the construction of a luxury golf-course, near Biot. Mention should be made of Marineland, 4 km from Antibes, Europe's leading attraction of this type, where dolphins, killer whales, seals, sea-lions, etc. perform.

The Naval and Napoleonic Museum. («Musée de la Marine, Paris»)

The beaches.

The promenade at
Golfe-Juan.

Part of Golfe-Juan harbour.

JUAN-LES-PINS

The elegant and modern structure of this spa is a pro-
longation of the city of Antibes and stretches beyond
the cape of the same name. Juan-les-Pins was founded by the American millionaire F.J. Gould and since
1925 has grown considerably in importance.

The beach, with its fine sand, is ideal for water sports,
and is the main tourist attraction of Juan-les-Pins. It is
enclosed by a mole which displays a profusion of
plants and flowers among which the terraces of the
Casino stand out, overlooking the sea, from which
there are magnificent views of the Golfe Juan, the
Island of Ste Marguerite and the Esterel.

Part of Juan-les-Pins.

Panorama of Vallauris.

VALLAURIS

Vallauris is an important pottery centre. Its name is linked with that of Picasso in the 20th century. Picasso who, having settled in Vallauris after the Second World War, injected new creative blood into local ceramic and pottery-work and in doing so renewed it. Picasso donated a group sculpture called *Man with Lamb* to Vallauris, which is placed in the Place Paul Isnard, and he also painted the monumental murals of *War and Peace* in the Romanesque chapel.

The Gallo-Romans had already made use of the substantial deposits of clay in the district, but the true tradition of ceramics and pottery in Vallauris began at the beginning of the 16th century, when the town, which had been decimated by the plague, was resettled by 70 families coming from the Genoese Riviera. Several of these new settlers began to manufacture domestic pottery utensils. The making of artistic objects began in the middle of the 19th century. Jacques Messier was one of the great masters of this art. From that time onwards production rose and ceramists of well-earned fame came on the scene, the most outstanding being Louis Pezzeto, Lévy Dhumes, Charles Lévêque and Father Sauvan. This corporation experienced remarkable development in the latter years of the 19th century, and, after a period of decline, Picasso infused new life into the ceramics of Vallauris. At present there are some 200 workshops.

Vallauris: Man with sheep, *by Picasso; the castle; and samples of craft work.*

The Town Hall of Le Cannet.

Le Cannet: Sainte-Philomène church.

LE CANNET - ROCHEVILLE

An important city which enjoys a privileged situation surrounded by hills. The sea breezes which reach Le Cannet arrive there after being made milder by the distance and the vegetation, and they are veritable caresses of the climate. Le Cannet was founded by the monks of Lérins and is one of those places most appreciated by lovers of peace and quiet.

Under the shelter of the Pézou and the Tête de Guillet, which rise to over 250 metres in height, there spread residential districts which make up what is known as Rocheville. Here the Provençal landscape of gardens and pine woods is maintained in the wide open spaces surrounding the modern buildings. The city has conserved various remnants of its distinguished history, amongst which the most important are the church of Saint Catherine, the chapels of Notre-Dame-des-Anges and Des Pénitents, the Tour des Brigands (15th century) and the Tour des Calvis. It is in Le Cannet that numerous distinguished personalities have their summer residence, and the city was the birthplace of father Ardisson (1660-1731), organiser of the defence against the troops of Eugene of Savoy. Likewise A.-L. Sardou, historian and father of the well-known writer Victorian Sardou, was born here. In Le Cannet too it was that the tragically famous Rachel died; here also lived the painters Pierre Bonnard and Henri Labasque. The Aga Khan built a villa which dominates the city.

MOUGINS

Mougins is situated at a height of 245 metres, between Cannes and Grasse, and is an ancient fortified town which has an attractively picturesque outline. It was occupied by the Ligurians and later conquered by the Romans. The origin of its name is a matter of controversy among historians. For some it is a derivation of *Mons Aighitnae,* while others believe it comes from *Mons Geminus.*

Mougins belonged to the abbey of Lérins and played an important historical role in the Middle Ages. The only remaining vestiges of its illustrious past are its walls and a fortified gate of the 15th century. The main monument is the parish church, construction of which was begun in the 11th century. From its belfry there is a beautiful sweeping view stretching from the Esterel to the Lérins islands and as far as the foothills of the Alps. In the Place Ste.-Anne there stands a monument to the memory of commander Lamy, a famous son of the town, who died a glorious death in Africa in 1900 on the banks of the Chari.

The chapel of Notre-Dame-de-Vie is ten minutes from Mougins. It is an old sanctuary, founded in the 12th century, and is surrounded by cypresses. Because of its privileged climatic situation, the monks of St. Honoré decided to make the spot a place of retreat. During the Middle Ages, Notre-Dame-de-Vie was one of the most important centres of pilgrimage in Provence.

Today Mougins is a tourist centre of no little importance, but the people have managed to retain their steady pace of living with their handsome Provence-style houses, white-walled and red-roofed, and with their luxurious parks which offer the attractive view of their terrace work. In Mougins there are several establishments which deservedly figure high on the list of any *gourmet.*

A picturesque corner.

Mougins: close-up of a fountain.

Grasse: the distillery and the laboratory of the Molinard Perfumery; a lavander field inland.

GRASSE

Grasse began its transformation into a tourist centre of note in the 19th century. Being the picturesque and welcoming city that it is, with the added attraction of a privileged site, it became the famous resort it is today.

The most important monument in Grasse is the cathedral of Notre-Dame, built in the 12th century and restored in the 17th century. It is built of reddish stone. The double access stairway (with a wide balustrade) and the crypts were added in the 18th century. In the interior of the church are conserved three paintings by Rubens, the *Lavatorium* by Fragonard, *The Mystical Betrothal of Saint Catherine,* a picture by Sebastian Bourdon, and the extraordinary altar-piece attributed to Louis Bréa.

The Place aux Aires, with its attractive porticoes, buildings displaying 18th-century façades, and its fine fountain, is the nerve centre of Grasse, together with the market. Some of the attractive sights in the place are the Jardin de la Princesse Pauline, the Hôpital du Petit Paris (in whose chapel there are three paintings by Natoire) and the Municipal park of La Corniche.

The economic life of Grasse has been determined for centuries now by the influence of perfumery. It is the world capital of the industry. Though the distillation of essences began back in the 13th century, the industrialisation of perfumery was initiated proper when the Medici family introduced the fashion of perfumed gloves in the 16th century. Nowadays some 10,000 tons of flowers are distilled each year, and the essential oils are used in the manufacture of the different essences used in perfumery.

Of interest in Grasse is the Musée Fragonard, dedicated to the memory of that painter who was born in the capital of perfumery (1732-1806). It is housed in a magnificent 18th-century building which once belonged to the Marchioness of Cabris, some of whose furniture still remains. In several of the rooms there are on display paintings with erotic themes (rejected by Madame du Barry) and which Fragonard hid in Grasse in the times of the French Revolution.

Grasse: Museum of Art and History (ceramic pieces); Fragonard Museum (a portrait of J.H. Fragonard and the 18th/19th century room).

Panorama of Cannes.

Photograph HELIFLASH

CANNES

The visitor will find Cannes on the site of an old Ligurian city giving onto the Golfe (Gulf) de La Napoule, with the Estérel massif rising behind the city: an incomparable location.

This privileged city amongst all those on the Côte d'Azur, then, is sheltered by a group of hills and enjoys a mild, temperature climate. As well as a centre for world-famous festivals, Cannes is nowadays one of the most attractive and highly frequented resorts in the world, where the tourist can enjoy the pleasures of the most elegant sports.

The city's origins are unknown because its history was anonymous for centuries until 1834, when Lord Brougham, former Lord Chancellor of Great Britain, was held up there on his way to Italy due to an epidemic of cholera. So impressed was he by the mild climate, the azure sky and the beauty of the area that he decided to build a house in Cannes, and returned there every winter.

Many other aristocrats followed Lord Brougham's example (he had also obtained from King Louis Philippe the funds necessary for the construction of a jetty next to the old town); Cannes expanded over the years, becoming a world-renowned tourist resort.

Up to 1834 it hat been no more than a tranquil fishing village whose history was closely connected with that of the Lérins Islands, Sainte-Marguerite and Saint-Honorat, which stand off the coast here. One of these

The Festival Palace and a view of the pleasure port.

Monument to Lord Brougham.

islands would seem to have had an important trading port and to have been a centre of pagan worship. Some historians believe that Cannes may have been a small fortified town which was destroyed by the Romans when they conquered the Côte d'Azur.

According to Polybius, the Greek historian, about two centuries before the Christian era the area around Cannes was inhabited by the Oxibians, a tribe made up of farmers and fishermen-cum-pirates: courageous, primitive workers. Polybius says that the Oxibians' capital, Egitna, stood on the site of what is now modern Cannes. This people attacked Antipolis — modern-day Antibes — and Nice, both colonies of Marseilles, and this Greek city appealed to the Romans to help reconquer and destroy Egitna.

In 155 BC Marseilles built the *Castrum Marcellinum* on this site, although some historians state that its construction dates from the Middle Ages. The Emperor Marcus Salvius Otto's troops subsequently engaged battle with those of Vitellius on the exact spot where Saint-Cassien chapel was later built in memory of Cassius, who was the first to occupy the position for which the two armies struggled fiercely. Several centuries later, when Christianity had already reached the Côte d'Azur, two anchorite monks, Honorat and Capraïs, took refuge in the Estérel mountains, then on the islands of Lero and Lérina, nowadays Sainte-Marguerite and Saint-Honorat. Popular legend has it that the second island was invaded by serpents, incarnations of the devil under the command of a fearsome dragon. Thanks to divine assistance, however, Honorat was able to invoke a tremendous tidal wave which destroyed the monsters in the depths of the sea. The hermit climbed a palm-tree in order to escape from the furious waves, this is why the monks' coat of arms bears two palm-leaves enclosing a golden crozier, whiles Cannes' arms have a silver palm-leaf set against a bar and blue ground. The Saracens invaded the region of Cannes in the first half of the 8th century and remained there for some years.

The gambling room of the Palm-Beach Hotel; and the Carlton Hotel.

In 990 Guillaume Gruetta, the Count of Antibes' second son, took possession of the Lérins Islands and made over to the Abbey his hands in Mandelieu, Arluc, Loubet and Cannes. The territory belonging to the island monks grew and, with the Pope's approval, became an autonomous feudal domain of considerable size. The Saracens nonetheless still occupied the fortress; Abbot Adalbert II converted the monastery into a stronghold and consolidated Cannes' defences by building the Tour du Suquet, which still exists today, on Mont-Chevalier.

Raymond Bérenguer, Count of Provence, granted charters to Cannes and a deed of 1131 confirms his donation of the *Castrum Marcellinum* (which became the *Castrum de Canoïs* as from 1200) to the Abbot of the Lérins. Despite various attempts at autonomy, Cannes continued to depend on the Lérins Monastery, which controlled the coastline from La Napoule to Vallauris. The monastery's decline dates from the 16th century, it arose from the king's granting the former ecclesiastical domain of the Islands to Prince Joinville, the Duke of Vendôme and other great lords.

After Provence lost its independence, towards the end of the 15th century, the castle at Cannes was occupied by Louis XI's troops. In 1580 two thirds of the population died in an epidemic of the plague. From 1635 to 1637 there were conflicts between the French and Spanish in the area: the latter conquered the Lérins Islands but were repulsed when they tried to land on the coast of Provence.

Fort Royal was built on Sainte-Marguerite Island at the time of Cardinal Richeliu, it dominates the marvellous panorama of Cannes, Antibes and the nearby hills. Fort Royal is where, from 1687 to 1698, the mysterious personage who has gone down in history as the "Man in the Iron Mask" was imprisoned. The visitor can view the chains which secured this legendary prisoner, whose identity remains an enigma.

Some historians have made hypotheses, with greater

The picturesque Rue Meynadier and a view of the Boulevard Carnot.

Midi and Gazagnaire beaches.

or lesser foundation, as to the Iron Mask's identity; and writers, among them Alexandre Dumas, author of ''The Three Musketeers,'' have given free rein to their imagination in their attempts to solve this mystery. Was the prisoner really Louis XIV's bastard brother, a son of Cromwell, the Duke of Beaufort, Fouquet's valet named Eustache Dauger?... The historical secret remains closed.

In the 18th century Cannes suffered various attacks by Arab pirates and invasion by the Duke of Savoy's troops, then by the Austrian army; the township was completely destroyed. In 1815 Napoleon fled from Elba and disembarked at Golfe-Juan. A small group of forty grenadiers, commanded by Cambronne, occupied Cannes and Napoleon was isolated in the midst of the dunes: he had to bivouac near the old chapel of Notre-Dame-du-Bon-Voyage before continuing up towards Paris.

Nineteen years later an English aristocrat, Lord Brougham, entered the history of Cannes, marking the starting point of the city's touristic facet.

The writer Prosper Mérimée — then an inspector of historical monuments — visited the Lérins Islands in 1858 and emphasised the importance of Cannes and its environs. After Mérimée, considered the second pioneer to discover the city's charm, came Guy de Maupassant, Tocqueville, Thiers, Victor Cousin, Stephen Liègeard and many other personalities of the arts and literature.

From this period onwards Cannes became one of the preferred haunts of artists, rich bankers, aristocrats and high-class tourists.

The image of modern Cannes is known the world over; the famous festivals — of records and the music industry in January, and the Film Festival in May — arouse the interest of the international press and draw music and cinema enthusiasts. Furthermore, numerous congresses and intense touristic activity make Cannes a fashionable city all the year round, thanks to a highly international clientèle.

The sports and leisure facilities of a city also enable

one to calibrate its dynamism and capacity to be ahead of the times. Without forsaking its traditional *fêtes,* Cannes endeavours to offer the numerous visitors new activities and installations: a port for pleasure-boats, golf courses, polo, water-sports, a flying-club, regattas, etc…

Cannes' flower is mimosa, which is exported all over the world; every year the mimosa festival is held in February, the flowering season.

Cannes extends over nine kilometres between the La Bocca quarter and the rocks of La Fourcade. There is a magnificent view of the city itself from the sea. The

Rue Meynadier, a paradise for gourmets.

The old fishing-port and the fish-market. ▷

A fountain and old shrine at Le Suquet.

centre is around the Rue d'Antibes, the Allées de la Liberté and, in particular, La Croisette. This promenade skirts the bay for three kilometres: a boulevard for the whole world running from the Old Port and the Palais des Congrès standing on the site of the old Municipal Casino, to Palm-Beach headland, where the Summer Casino and Port Canto are to be found. The city is truly a spectacle, unfolding in a framework of sea, golden sand, flowers and palm-trees. The Hôtel Carlton stands at the centre of La Croisette, like a symbol of Cannes' soaring vocation. The concentration of large hotels around the Congress and Festival Palace, the luxury apartment blocks, shops bearing the foremost names in fashion, the huge esplanade won back from the sea and planted with pleasant gardens: all these are invaluable attractions for the city.

The Boulevard Carnot extends Cannes to the north as far as Le Cannet. To the west, the Boulevard Jean Hibert skirts the Plage du Midi ("South Beach") as far as La Bocca; whereas the eastern side is composed of handsome avenues leading to the luxurious residential areas of La Californie and Cannes-Eden.

The Rue d'Antibes, which runs parallel to La Croisette, is a very important shopping area, with excellent stores. We should also mention the bustling activity of the more typical Rue Meynadier, with crowds of customers weaving through the displays. In the centre of the old town, on top of Le Suquet hill, is the little Place de la Castre, delimited to the north by remains of the 14th-century ramparts. This is a contemplative spot, shaded by pines and ennobled by an interesting 16th-century church (whose structure is reminiscent of Gothic architecture) with several polychrome statues.

Discovering the panorama over Cannes from the ancient walls of Le Suquet is a magnificent spectacle. Le Suquet is the old *Castrum de Canoïs,* the streets and houses cluster together on the slopes of Mont Chevalier. The physiognomy of Le Suquet displays the intimate character of a village, in contrast with the

Interior and bell-tower of the church of Notre-Dame de l'Epérance; and a detail of one of the galleries in the Musée de la Castre.

exalted life of modern Cannes. Here all is tranquil, silent. The Tour du Suquet is a tower 22 m. high which was built by the monks from the Lérins Islands, it is one of the most representative monuments of old Cannes. The Tower was destroyed during the French Revolution but later restored on the initiative of the fishermen of Cannes since they used it as a landmark for coastal navigation.

The old urban quarter of Le Suquet rises above the ancient port. The streets are picturesque and winding: Rues du Mont-Chevalier, de Saint-Antoine, de la Boucherie, du Pré, de Saint-Dizier… The church of Notre-Dame de l'Espérance is to be found within the

Three aspects of the important Musée de la Castre.

area of Le Suquet; finished in the meridional Gothic style in 1645, it houses some quite fine retables from the classical era, beautiful 17th-century reliquary busts, a superb large 16th-century Virgin Mary on the high altar and the remarkable statue of St. Anne, also dating from the 16th century.

The Musée de la Castre is located on the Place de la Castre and houses extremely diverse collections and exhibits: an Etruscan sarcophagus of the Hellenic era, two lead sarcophagi found at Sidon, a painted sar-cophagus bearing the name of Imenhetep, the scribe (20th dynasty), pre-Columbian ceramics, Polynesian ethnography, pottery from Asia Minor and Rhodes, Egyptian antiquities, anchors, amphoras, funeral objects from the region, etc…

This museum was founded with the collections of a rich Dutch baron, Lycklama: there is a portrait of him, dressed in Oriental style, in one of the rooms.

After La Californie, the residential area of Cannes, there appear the superb hills of Super-Cannes. From

The Quai Saint-Pierre and Le Suquet by moonlight.

them there is a splendid view of the countryside extending from the Esteral to the Italian border. The Avenue Isola-Bella and the Rue de A.-L. Sardou lead to the Observatory.

The Observatory tower and a panoramic view of Super-Cannes.

The Monastery of the Lérins Islands.

ILES DE LERINS

There have always been close historical links between Cannes and the Lérins islands, and today relations have become tourist orientated. Most noteworthy are the spectacles of sound and light of great resonance and extraordinary quality, which are held throughout the summer. Cannes is linked to the islands by a constant boat service which enables one to take a leisurely trip around a highly attractive sea.

Sainte-Marguerite is the largest of the Iles de Lérins as well as being the highest. It stretches for three kilometres from east to west, and is approximately 900 metres wide. Except for the grounds of the Domaine du Grand Jardin, Sainte-Marguerite belongs to the French state. The island has a beautiful population of pine and eucaliptus woods, criss-crossed with beautiful avenues. There is a small group of fishermen living on Sainte-Marguerite and it also has a few shops.

Its name comes from the sister of St. Honorat, Marguerite, who founded a convent on the island in the 5th century. During its history, the convent was occupied by Visigoths, Ostrogoths and the Franks. The island had previously been conquered by the Romans. For many centuries Sainte-Marguerite belonged to the monks of Lérins. At the beginning of the 17th century it was ceded first of all to the Duke of Chevreuse then to the the Duke of Guise and finally to Jean de Bellon. At about this time work on a fort was

begun, and this fort today houses the Museum of the Sea.

The stronghold was built by Richelieu and reinforced by Vauban. In 1687, being a State prison, the lord of Saint-Mars had in his custody the mysterious personage known as the "Iron Mask" (d. 1703), whom he took with him as prisoner when he obtained the post as governor of the Bastille in 1698. The room where the enigmatic character was imprisoned still stands, as well as the cells in which the French protestant pastors were imprisoned after the revocation of the Edict of Nantes. The castle, from the terrace of which there is a magnificently beautiful view of the coast, with the first peaks of the Alps in the distance, was also the prison of Maréchal Bazaine for eight months until he managed to escape in August 1874. For eight hundred years Saint-Honorat was the seat of the monks who governed Cannes and its surrounding area. In 575 the monks adopted the rule of Saint Benedict, though the monastery (which has suffered several attacks during its history) is at present occupied by monks belonging to the Cistercian order.

The vegetation on St.-Honorat is dense, with pines, bay trees, vineyards and flowers abounding. It is 1,500 metres long by 400 metres wide. Its coastline is lower and it is less welcoming than Sainte-Marguerite. The islands are separated by a narrow strait called the "Plateau du Milieu".

Though there are several interesting Romanesque chapels on St.-Honorat, the most important monument is the castle, built in the 11th century and rectangular in shape. It is a sort of fortified prison which rises on the same site as a Roman cistern. The castle was a refuge for the monks of Lérins during the numerous attacks which they had to suffer throughout the centuries.

The present monastery was built in the 19th century and has incorporated the old buildings occupied by previous monks.

The Museum is of interest. In it are conserved fragments of Roman and Christian tombstones alluding to its history and internal evolution.

Photograph HELIFLASH

La Bocca and the bay of La Napoule; and a beautiful sunset at La Bocca.

LA BOCCA

In 1834 the westernmost houses of Cannes were situated on the edge of the dunes and pine groves, there being only the Château and St-Cassien chapel in La Bocca. Joseph Barthélémy, a glassmaker, established himself there towards 1855 and originated the present-day urban agglomeration. Today, La Bocca is an important commercial and industrial centre, with its shipyards, repair workshops, etc... Sensibly developed housing estates have facilitated the construction of genuine villages at La Frayère, Le Bosquet, Fouéry and La Croix des Gardes.

La Napoule: the castle.

MANDELIEU - LA NAPOULE

This town has had a variety of names. The Romans called it *Mantolvocus, Mandolocas* or *Mandullocus.* In the Middle Ages the city was given its present name.

Eucher, Lord of Mandelieu, a learned and generous man, freed his slaves about the year 400 and distributed a large portion of his wealth amongst the villeins of his fief. In the 8th century the Saracens utterly destroyed the city. Only a few of its inhabitants managed to escape, and they then proceeded to rebuild it. In 1706 the new town (present-day Capitou) was built and in 1782 a new bridge was thrown across the Siagne. Towards the end of the 19th century a cork factory was erected in Les Termes, an event which doubled the number of inhabitants in the town. Gilbert Nabonnand, the famous horticulturalist of the Golfe-Juan, imported the mimosa from Australia and acclimatized it to the area, thus contributing to the enrichment of his city.

La Napoule, situated some 7 kilometres from Cannes, is Mandelieu's exit to the sea. The castle of La Napoule was built in 1390 by the lords of Villeneuve. It rises from rocks. The castle was destroyed by Raymond de Turenne and the only remains of its ruins are three solid square towers with their parapets. In 1919 it was restored by the American sculptor Henry Clews and today it houses the work of this same artist.

La Napoule has become a tourist centre of the first rank, thanks to its being a winter resort and spa and to its excellent beach of fine sand.

Photograph HELIFLASH ▷

La Napoule: interiors of the castle (Henry Clews Foundation); and the port.

◁ *The castle at La Napoule and a panaroma of the bay.*

La Croix-des-Gardes, view of Théoule and Port-la-Galère.

A view of the Mimosa Lake at Tanneron; and part of
Spéracèdes.

Saint-Cézaire-sur-Siagne: an aspect of the celebrated
grottoes.

SAINT-CEZAIRE-SUR-SIAGNE

Saint-Cézaire is a little village 15 km west of Grasse,
standing on the edge of a plateau overlooking the
Siagne; it has retained its feudal physiognomy, with
ruins of a castle and a 12th century Romanesque
chapel.

It is 500 m. above sea-level, the visitor will discover a
superb panorama embracing the Monts de Tanneron,
the Estérel, the Lérins Islands, Cannes and Mougins.
St-Cézaire's fame is due above all to the grottoes
discovered in the limestone in the last century. They
attain a depth of almost 50 m. underground, stretch
over 200 m. and enjoy a constant temperature of
14° C. These caves are remarkable for the variety and
richness of the calcareous formations, and for the
unimaginable fantasia which nature has deployed
over the centuries in this astounding creation. The
almost musical stalactites and stalagmites are notable
by virtue of their variety of forms (corals, stars,
flowers, animals) and also of the red tint caused by
the presence of iron oxide.

The pleasure port at Agay.

Splendid landscape overlooked by the Estérel.

Part of Saint-Raphaël.

Photograph HELIFLASH

The pleasure port at Sainte-Maxime-sur-Mer.

View of Saint-Tropez.

Overall view of the bay of St. Tropez and Grimaud.

Part of the port at
Saint-Tropez.

Tahiti, Beach.

Photograph HELIFLASH

*Aeirial view of the
Port at Saint-Tropez.*

Photograph HELIFLASH

Part of Le Lavandou.

Contents

Collection ALL EUROPE

#		Spanish	French	English	German	Italian	Catalan	Dutch	Swedish	Portuguese	Japanese	Finnish
1	ANDORRA	●	●	●	●	●	●					
2	LISBON	●	●	●	●	●				●		
3	LONDON	●	●	●	●	●					●	
4	BRUGES	●	●	●	●	●		●				
5	PARIS	●	●	●	●	●					●	
6	MONACO	●	●	●	●	●						
7	VIENNA	●	●	●	●	●						
11	VERDUN	●	●	●	●			●				
12	THE TOWER OF LONDON	●	●	●	●	●						
13	ANTWERP	●	●	●	●	●						
14	WESTMINSTER ABBEY	●	●	●	●	●						
15	THE SPANISH RIDING SCHOOL IN VIENNA	●	●	●	●	●						
16	FATIMA	●	●	●	●	●				●		
17	WINDSOR CASTLE	●	●	●	●	●					●	
19	COTE D'AZUR	●	●	●	●	●						
22	BRUSSELS	●	●	●	●	●		●				
23	SCHÖNBRUNN PALACE	●	●	●	●	●		●				
24	ROUTE OF PORT WINE	●	●	●	●	●				●		
26	HOFBURG PALACE	●	●	●	●	●						
27	ALSACE	●	●	●	●	●		●				
31	MALTA				●	●	●					
32	PERPIGNAN		●									
33	STRASBOURG											
34	MADEIRA + PORTO SANTO	●	●	●						●		
35	CERDAGNE - CAPCIR		●				●					
36	BERLIN	●	●	●	●	●						

Collection ART IN SPAIN

#		Spanish	French	English	German	Italian	Catalan	Dutch	Swedish	Portuguese	Japanese	Finnish
1	PALAU DE LA MUSICA CATALANA	●		●			●					
2	GAUDI	●	●	●	●						●	
3	PRADO MUSEUM I (Spanish Painting)	●	●	●	●	●					●	
4	PRADO MUSEUM II (Foreign Painting)	●	●	●	●	●						
5	MONASTERY OF GUADALUPE	●										
6	THE CASTLE OF XAVIER	●	●	●	●						●	
7	THE FINE ARTS MUSEUM OF SEVILLE	●	●	●	●	●						
8	SPANISH CASTLES	●	●	●		●						
9	THE CATHEDRALS OF SPAIN	●	●	●		●						
10	THE CATHEDRAL OF GERONA	●	●	●		●						
14	PICASSO	●	●	●	●						●	
15	REALES ALCAZARES (ROYAL PALACE OF SEVILLE)	●	●	●	●	●						
16	MADRID'S ROYAL PALACE	●	●	●	●	●						
17	ROYAL MONASTERY OF EL ESCORIAL	●	●	●	●	●						
18	THE WINES OF CATALONIA	●										
19	THE ALHAMBRA AND THE GENERALIFE	●	●	●	●	●						
20	GRANADA AND THE ALHAMBRA	●										
21	ROYAL ESTATE OF ARANJUEZ	●	●	●	●	●						
22	ROYAL ESTATE OF EL PARDO	●	●	●	●	●						
23	ROYAL HOUSES	●	●	●	●	●						
24	ROYAL PALACE OF SAN ILDEFONSO	●	●	●	●	●						
25	HOLY CROSS OF THE VALLE DE LOS CAIDOS	●	●	●	●	●						
26	OUR LADY OF THE PILLAR OF SARAGOSSA	●	●	●			●					
27	TEMPLE DE LA SAGRADA FAMILIA	●	●	●	●	●		●				
28	POBLET ABTEI	●	●	●		●		●				

Collection ALL SPAIN

#		Spanish	French	English	German	Italian	Catalan	Dutch	Swedish	Portuguese	Japanese	Finnish
1	ALL MADRID	●	●	●	●	●					●	
2	ALL BARCELONA	●	●	●	●	●	●					
3	ALL SEVILLE	●	●	●	●	●					●	
4	ALL MAJORCA	●	●	●	●	●						
5	ALL THE COSTA BRAVA	●	●	●	●	●						
6	ALL MALAGA and the Costa del Sol	●	●	●	●	●			●			
7	ALL THE CANARY ISLANDS (Gran Canaria)	●	●	●	●	●			●	●		
8	ALL CORDOBA	●	●	●	●	●					●	
9	ALL GRANADA	●	●	●	●	●					●	
10	ALL VALENCIA	●	●	●	●	●						
11	ALL TOLEDO	●	●	●	●	●					●	
12	ALL SANTIAGO	●	●	●	●	●						
13	ALL IBIZA and Formentera	●	●	●	●	●						
14	ALL CADIZ and the Costa de la Luz	●	●	●	●	●						
15	ALL MONTSERRAT	●	●	●	●	●						
16	ALL SANTANDER and Cantabria	●		●								
17	ALL THE CANARY ISLANDS II, (Tenerife)	●	●	●	●	●			●	●		●
20	ALL BURGOS	●	●	●	●	●						
21	ALL ALICANTE and the Costa Blanca	●	●	●	●	●			●			
22	ALL NAVARRA	●	●	●								
23	ALL LERIDA	●	●	●	●	●	●					
24	ALL SEGOVIA	●	●	●	●							
25	ALL SARAGOSSA	●	●	●	●							
26	ALL SALAMANCA	●	●	●	●	●			●			
27	ALL AVILA	●	●	●	●							
28	ALL MINORCA	●	●	●	●							
29	ALL SAN SEBASTIAN and Guipúzcoa	●										
30	ALL ASTURIAS	●			●							
31	ALL LA CORUNNA and the Rías Altas	●	●	●	●							
32	ALL TARRAGONA	●	●	●	●	●						
33	ALL MURCIA	●	●	●	●							
34	ALL VALLADOLID	●	●	●	●							
35	ALL GIRONA	●	●	●	●							
36	ALL HUESCA	●	●									
37	ALL JAEN	●	●	●	●							
38	ALL ALMERIA	●	●	●	●							
40	ALL CUENCA	●	●	●	●							
41	ALL LEON	●	●	●	●							
42	ALL PONTEVEDRA, VIGO and the Rías Bajas	●	●	●	●							
43	ALL RONDA	●	●	●	●							
44	ALL SORIA	●										
46	ALL EXTREMADURA											
47	ALL ANDALUSIA	●	●	●	●	●						
52	ALL MORELLA	●	●	●	●			●				

Collection ALL AMERICA

#		Spanish	French	English	German	Italian	Catalan	Dutch	Swedish	Portuguese	Japanese	Finnish
1	PUERTO RICO	●		●								
2	SANTO DOMINGO	●		●								
3	QUEBEC		●	●								
4	COSTA RICA	●										
5	CARACAS	●		●								

Collection ALL AFRICA

#		Spanish	French	English	German	Italian	Catalan	Dutch	Swedish	Portuguese	Japanese	Finnish
1	MOROCCO	●	●	●	●	●						
2	THE SOUTH OF MOROCCO	●	●	●	●	●						
3	TUNISIA			●	●	●						
4	RWANDA		●									

The printing of this book was completed
in the workshops of
FISA - ESCUDO DE ORO, S.A.
Palaudarias, 26 - Barcelona (Spain)